WILLIAMS-SONOMA

Fun Food

recipes
stephanie rosenbaum

general editor
chuck williams

photography
jason lowe

fP
FREE PRESS

NEW YORK · LONDON · TORONTO · SYDNEY

contents

✱ For a complete list of recipes, turn to page 128.

7

basics

51

oodles of noodles

69

put on your oven mitts

15
kid classics

35
after-school snacks

91
don't forget the veggies

105
time for a sandwich

hey kids!

This book shows you how fun and easy cooking can be! There are times when you need to pay attention, like when you are using knives, cooking on the stove top, and baking in the oven. But don't worry, all you need to remember are two key words: sharp and hot. Whenever those words come to mind, ask an adult to stand by. They can be really helpful (and may even wash the dishes!).

Here are some secrets to cooking success:

* Read the Basics section first.

* Before you begin any recipe, read it from start to finish.

* Look for the splats over the numbers in the recipe steps. These will tell you which picture goes with each step.

Beyond that, all that's left to do is to start cooking and have some fun!

hey parents!

The recipes in this cookbook are intended for kids age 8 and up, to use with as much independence as seems right for their age and skill level. Only you can gauge how much support you will need to give to your children as they cook. Help your children by reviewing the recipe with them before they begin and identifying any steps that may require adult supervision.

getting started

Before you begin to cook, make sure an adult is around to help out. If you have long hair, tie it back. Take off any dangling things, like scarves, hair ribbons, or jewelry that could catch on fire, fall into a pan, or get tangled. Roll up long sleeves and put on an apron.

clear your work surface

The next thing you need is a clean work surface. Before the fun begins, clear off a big, flat area, such as a kitchen counter or table, to work on. Wipe down the surface to make sure it's clean. Then, wash and dry your hands thoroughly.

assemble your supplies

In restaurants, chefs always get their equipment and ingredients ready before they start cooking. They call this their *mise en place* (pronounced MEEZ ahn plahse), meaning "everything in its place."

Take a look at the list of equipment and ingredients for the recipe you're making. Get out all your tools first. Then, get out all the ingredients you're going to need. Ingredients combine better at room temperature, so let cold items from the refrigerator warm up for no longer than 1 hour before using them, unless the recipe says otherwise.

Next, peel and chop your vegetables or fruits and measure out all your ingredients. If the recipe calls for using the oven, turn it on to the correct temperature before you start. To be sure your oven is at the right temperature, always "preheat" it for 10 to 15 minutes before you use it.

Many of the recipes in this book call for greasing a pan or dish before you fill it. This helps keep the food from sticking and makes cleanup easier. To do this, use a piece of paper towel to swab a small amount of softened butter or a little oil, then rub it all over on the bottom of the pan and up the sides.

preparing ingredients

washing fruits & vegetables

Wash all produce under slightly warm running water. Scrub root vegetables, such as potatoes, with a soft brush to remove any dirt. If you have several items to wash at once, put them into a colander and rinse them together.

peeling & trimming produce

To peel firm fruits and vegetables, hold the item to be peeled in one hand. With the other hand, peel off the skin with a vegetable peeler, always moving the peeler away from you. Try to take off only the peel, leaving as much of the flesh as you can. With a sharp knife, trim off any tough or dirty stems and root ends. If you see any brown spots or bruises, cut them off.

grating & shredding

To shred or grate, hold a box grater-shredder firmly on top of a plate or cutting board. Rub the item against the holes of the grater-shredder, keeping your fingers away from the sharp holes. The smallest holes, which are raised and resemble small metal teeth, are used for grating. These will make tiny particles of citrus zest or hard cheese. The larger oval holes, used for shredding, will make short and fine or long and coarse pieces of soft cheese. You may need to chop the last bit with a knife to avoid grating or shredding fingers.

cracking eggs

To crack an egg, tap it firmly on a flat surface until the shell cracks. Holding one end of the egg with each hand, pull the shell halves apart over a small, clean bowl until the egg drops out into the bowl. Throw away the shell. Next, check for shell fragments: If a piece of shell drops into the bowl, chase it to the side of the bowl with a spoon and then lift it out. Pour the egg into the mixing bowl.

of ¼ teaspoon, ½ teaspoon, 1 teaspoon, and 1 tablespoon. The same spoons are used for wet and dry ingredients.

how to measure dry ingredients

To measure dry ingredients such as flour, spoon the ingredient into the correct-sized dry measuring cup. Do not pack down the ingredient (unless it's brown sugar, which is measured firmly packed). Using the flat side of a table knife, sweep off the excess even with the rim. Loose dry ingredients, such as raisins, can be scooped into dry measuring cups. Fill the cup but don't pack it tightly unless the recipe says to. To measure small amounts of dry ingredients, dip the correct-sized measuring spoon into the ingredient, then use the back of a table knife to sweep off the excess.

how to measure liquids

To measure liquid ingredients such as milk or water, set a clear liquid measuring cup on a flat surface, like a countertop. Pour the liquid into the cup. Now, scoot down so that your face is level with the cup and look at the measuring line for the amount you need. Does the level of the liquid match the correct line? If not, add more liquid (or pour some out) until the two lines are even. To measure a small amount of liquid, carefully pour the ingredient into a measuring spoon until it reaches the rim.

measuring

The recipes in this book will tell you how much of an ingredient you will need, then tell you whether you need to peel, chop, or grate it. Always use standard measuring cups and spoons for measuring. If an ingredient, such as salt, is listed without an amount, it means you should taste and decide for yourself how much of the ingredient is needed.

types of measuring tools

Dry and wet ingredients are measured in cups and spoons. Measuring cups for dry ingredients are made of metal or plastic and usually come in sets of ¼, ⅓, ½, and 1 cup. Measuring cups for liquid ingredients are made from clear glass or plastic, with the measurements marked on the sides. Measuring spoons typically come in sets

knife skills

Whenever you're going to use a knife, ask an adult to help you. Always make sure your knife is sharp. Sharp knives are safer than dull knives because they cut cleanly and easily. You need to use a lot of pressure to cut with a dull knife, and it's more likely to slip or get stuck in what you're cutting. (You can hurt yourself with sharp knives too, of course, so use them with care.)

about cutting boards

Use a cutting board, made from wood or plastic, every time you cut. Other surfaces may be slippery, or they may dull your knife.

It's best to keep two cutting boards, one for fruits and vegetables and one for raw meat, poultry, and fish, to avoid spreading germs.

how to use a knife

✱ Choose a knife that fits comfortably in your hand and doesn't feel too big. Your hands are much smaller than an adult's, so you can do the same jobs they do with a smaller tool.

✱ Hold the knife firmly by the handle. You can extend your index finger along the top or side of the blade to help guide the knife.

✱ Hold down the item you are cutting with your other hand, placing the food on a flat side whenever you can. (You can even cut a little slice off a round item if you like.)

✱ Curl under the fingers of the hand that's holding the food to keep them out of harm's way. You can use your knuckles as a shield to keep the blade from coming too close to your fingertips.

✱ Start to cut, always moving the knife away from your body as you do. The recipe will tell you whether to cut crosswise (across) or lengthwise (along the length).

food safety

Keeping the food you cook safe and healthful is mostly a matter of common sense. As your parents tell you: Always wash your hands with hot water and soap before you start cooking, after you finish, and frequently in the middle. Also, don't forget to wash before you sit down to eat.

keeping things clean & safe

Raw meat, chicken, fish, and eggs can contain bacteria that will make you sick.

To prevent these types of raw foods from contaminating cooked foods or uncooked fruits and vegetables, make sure you promptly wash any plates, bowls, cutting boards, knives, and other utensils you used with hot, soapy water. Remember to wash your hands thoroughly at the same time. Also, never taste raw meats or poultry, and be sure to discard any paper or plastic wrappings that came with the meats, poultry, or fish as soon as possible.

Here are some more helpful hints for keeping your treats fresh and delicious:

✳ Never taste raw eggs, as they can sometimes contain bacteria that will make you sick. It's a good idea to wash your hands again each time you touch raw eggs.

✳ Germs, better known as bacteria, grow best in warm temperatures, so always keep hot foods hot and cold foods cold.

✳ Put things away as you go. Don't leave ingredients that should be refrigerated sitting out on the counter for more than 1 hour (less in hot weather).

✳ Don't put hot food straight into the refrigerator. This will raise the temperature in the refrigerator and may cause other foods stored there to spoil. Instead, let the hot food cool to room temperature before putting it into the fridge.

clean up as you cook

Good cooks know it's important to clean up as you go along. Don't save it all until the end. Put a dirty spoon in the sink or dishwasher instead of leaving it on the countertop. After you measure out an ingredient, put it away. Keep a clean dish towel or sponge handy for spills. Wipe down your work surface or cutting board often, and wash your hands whenever they get sticky.

start cooking!

Before you turn on the stove or the oven, double-check to make sure an adult is nearby. Ask them to find you a sturdy chair or stool that you can safely stand on, so that you can see what's going on.

Cooking on the stove top or in the oven can sometimes seem scary. But don't let the fear stop you! Keep these final tips in mind and you'll be well on your way to cooking with confidence.

tips for working with hot things

✳ Always angle pot handles toward the back of the stove so you won't knock a pot off the stove by mistake. Never reach over an open flame.

✳ Never leave something cooking on the stove top unattended. If you need to leave the kitchen, be sure to turn off the burner and remove the pan from the heat.

✳ If you need to leave the kitchen while the oven is still on, be sure to let an adult know your plans.

✳ To protect your hands when working with hot items, always use clean, dry pot holders or oven mitts (oven mitts are nice because they act like gloves). Wet oven mitts will not protect you.

✳ Ask an adult to help you take large, hot pots off the stove. Have an adult help you take heavy pans out of the oven, too.

✳ Tilt the lid away from you as you lift it off a hot pan. Steam is hotter than boiling water, which means it can burn you.

✳ Burners, especially electric ones, stay hot even after they are turned off. Never put anything that might get burnt onto a burner, including paper towels, cookbooks, oven mitts, or, of course, your hands.

✳ The inside of the oven door and the oven racks are very hot, so be careful not to touch them when checking or removing your finished food.

✳ Remember to set a timer when you're cooking. It's easy to get distracted by other things while your pasta is boiling, so don't rely on your memory to remind you when the food will be ready.

✳ Have a heatproof trivet, tile, or cooling rack ready on a flat surface before you take a hot pan out of the oven. Let hot pots and pans cool before putting them in the sink or cleaning them up.

✳ Remember to turn off the burner or oven after you are finished using it.

✳ Finally, remember to work slowly so you will avoid making mistakes.

You are now ready to choose a recipe and begin to cook. One last thing before you start: Above all, remember to have fun!

kid
classics

macaroni & cheese

ingredients

butter 2 tablespoons

all-purpose flour 2 tablespoons

whole milk 1½ cups

salt 2½ teaspoons

ground nutmeg 2 big pinches

ground pepper 2 big pinches

white or yellow Cheddar cheese 2 cups shredded (8 ounces)

grated Parmesan cheese 2 tablespoons

elbow macaroni ½ pound

tools

measuring cups & spoons

box grater-shredder

medium & large saucepans or pots

whisk

wooden spoon

oven mitts

long-handled wooden fork

colander

1 melt the butter

✻ Before you start, be sure an adult is nearby to help.

✻ Put the butter in the medium saucepan. Place the saucepan over low heat and warm until the butter is melted.

2 add the flour

✻ Add the flour to the melted butter. Using the whisk, stir the flour and butter together until the mixture is smooth and bubbling but not browned, about 1 minute.

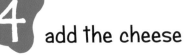

3 add the milk & cook

✳ Raise the heat under the saucepan to medium. While stirring constantly with the wooden spoon, slowly pour the milk into the saucepan.

✳ Continue to stir and cook until the mixture is smooth, thickened, and gently bubbling, 6–8 minutes. It should be about as thick as melted ice cream.

4 add the cheese

✳ Wearing oven mitts, remove the saucepan from the heat.

✳ Add ½ teaspoon of the salt, the nutmeg, and the pepper. Stir several times, then add the Cheddar and Parmesan cheeses. Stir until the cheeses have melted and the sauce is smooth.

✳ Cover the saucepan with the lid to keep the sauce warm and set it aside.

5 boil water

✳ Fill the large saucepan three-quarters full with water. Place over high heat and bring to a rolling boil.

✳ When the water is boiling, add the remaining 2 teaspoons salt.

6 cook the macaroni

✴ Pour the macaroni into the boiling water. Wait a minute, then stir and push the macaroni down into the water with the wooden fork.

✴ Boil the macaroni, uncovered, stirring occasionally, until tender but not mushy, 7–8 minutes, or according to the directions on the package.

7 drain the macaroni

✴ Set the colander in the sink.

✴ Ask an adult to help you pour the macaroni into the colander. Let the macaroni drain, shaking the colander a few times to shake off the extra water.

8 coat with the sauce

✴ Add the drained macaroni to the saucepan with the cheese sauce. Using the wooden fork, stir the macaroni until it is well coated with the cheese sauce.

✴ Spoon the macaroni and cheese into bowls and serve right away.

chicken noodle soup

ingredients

chicken broth 4 cups

water 2 cups

boneless, skinless chicken breast halves 2

carrot 1

celery 1 rib

garlic 1 clove

dried thyme, dill, or parsley ½ teaspoon

salt

short egg noodles 1½ cups (3 ounces)

tools

measuring cups & spoons

tongs

large saucepan or pot

oven mitts

cutting board

sharp knife

paring knife

plate

vegetable peeler

metal spatula

wooden spoon

ladle

1 boil the broth & water

✱ Before you start, be sure an adult is nearby to help.

✱ Combine the chicken broth and water in the saucepan. Place over medium heat and bring to a boil.

2 cook the chicken

✱ Use the tongs to add the chicken pieces to the saucepan and turn the heat down to low so that the liquid is gently bubbling. This is called simmering.

✱ Simmer the chicken, uncovered, until it is cooked through, 10–12 minutes.

✱ To test if the chicken is done, remove a piece of chicken with the tongs, put it on the cutting board, and cut into it with the paring knife. It should be firm and white all the way through.

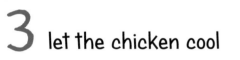

3 let the chicken cool

✳ Turn off the heat under the saucepan.

✳ Using the tongs, lift the chicken pieces out of the broth and put them on the plate. Set aside to cool.

✳ Leave the pan of broth sitting on the stove top with the heat turned off.

✳ While the chicken cools, continue with steps 4–7.

4 dice the carrot

✳ Using the vegetable peeler, peel the carrot. Put the carrot on the cutting board and, using the knife, cut off the stem end.

✳ Cut the carrot crosswise into 3 pieces. Cut each piece in half lengthwise. Then lay each piece flat side down and cut in half again lengthwise. You'll have 12 sticks.

✳ A few at a time, stack the sticks into a pile. Hold the stack of sticks together with one hand. With your other hand, cut the sticks crosswise into small cubes. Watch your fingers!

5 dice the celery

✳ Using the knife, cut off the top and bottom of the celery stalk.

✳ Cut the celery stalk crosswise into 3 pieces. Cut each piece in half lengthwise. Then cut each piece in half again lengthwise. You'll have 12 sticks.

✳ A few at a time, stack the sticks into a pile. Hold the stack of sticks together with one hand. With your other hand, cut the sticks crosswise into small cubes. Watch your fingers!

6 slice the garlic

✳ Put the garlic clove on the cutting board. Place the flat part of the metal spatula over the garlic clove and press down hard with the heel of your palm to break and loosen the papery skin. Don't worry if you smash the garlic a little.

✳ Peel off the skin and throw it away. Use the paring knife to cut the garlic into 4 or 5 slices.

7 simmer the vegetables

✳ Put the carrot, celery, garlic, and thyme into the saucepan with the chicken broth and stir with the wooden spoon.

✳ Turn on the heat to medium and heat the broth until small bubbles form on the surface of the broth.

✳ Let the vegetables cook until softened, about 10 minutes. Taste the broth (careful, it's hot!) and season with salt if you think it needs some.

8 shred the chicken

✳ When the chicken is cool enough to handle, use your fingers or the knife to pull or cut it into bite-sized shreds or pieces.

✳ Add the shredded chicken back to the simmering soup along with the egg noodles. Cook until the noodles are tender but not mushy, about 5 minutes.

✳ Ladle the soup into bowls. Serve right away.

more ideas!

Asian chicken soup

Follow the recipe for Chicken Noodle Soup but add 2 thick slices peeled fresh ginger to the broth in step 1. Replace the egg noodles in step 8 with 3 ounces Asian rice vermicelli and add 1 tablespoon soy sauce at the same time. Pick out the ginger slices with tongs before you serve the soup. Garnish each bowl of soup with chopped fresh basil or mint.

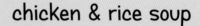

chicken & rice soup

Follow the recipe for Chicken Noodle Soup but replace the noodles with ⅓ cup uncooked long-grain rice. Add the rice to the saucepan with the broth and the water in step 1, then follow the recipe as directed for the chicken and vegetables.

tortilla soup

Follow the recipe for Chicken Noodle Soup but leave out the noodles. In step 8, add ½ cup tortilla chips, broken into pieces, to the saucepan along with the shredded chicken. Cook for 1 minute. Cut 1 lime in half and squeeze the juice into the soup just before serving. If you like, garnish each bowl of soup with a few avocado chunks and a spoonful of sour cream.

in Mexico, tortilla chips replace the noodles in chicken soup

sesame fish sticks

ingredients

halibut, cod, or other firm white fish fillets 1½ pounds

all-purpose flour 1 cup

salt ¼ teaspoon

ground pepper ¼ teaspoon

large eggs 2

sesame seeds 1 cup

vegetable oil ¼ cup

lemon wedges for serving

tartar sauce or tomato ketchup for serving

tools

measuring cups & spoons

cutting board

sharp knife

3 shallow pans or dishes

fork

3 plates

paper towels

sauté pan

tongs or metal spatula

baking dish

oven mitts

1 cut the fish sticks

✳ Before you start, be sure an adult is nearby to help.

✳ Put the fish fillets on the cutting board. Using the knife, cut the fish fillets into sticks measuring about 1 by 5 inches. Transfer to a plate and set aside.

2 get ready to coat

✳ Pour the flour into one of the shallow pans. Sprinkle the salt and pepper over the flour and stir with the fork until blended.

✳ Crack the eggs into another shallow pan, then beat the eggs with the fork until they are smooth and uniformly yellow.

✳ Pour the sesame seeds into the last shallow pan.

✳ Line up the pans of flour, eggs, and sesame seeds in a row in front of you, in that order.

✳ If the food doesn't sizzle when it goes into the pan, your oil isn't hot enough for frying.

✳ Heat the oil for 20–30 seconds more, then drop a tiny piece of bread in to see if it sizzles. Remove the bread before cooking the fish.

solved!

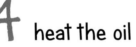

3 coat the fish sticks

✳ Drag a fish piece through the flour, turning to coat it all over. Gently shake off the extra flour.

✳ Now dip the fish piece quickly into the eggs, letting the excess drip off.

✳ Finally, drag the fish piece through the sesame seeds, turning it to coat evenly with the seeds. Set it aside on a clean plate.

✳ Repeat until you have coated all the fish pieces.

4 heat the oil

✳ Place a layer of paper towels on the last clean plate.

✳ Get an adult to help you now. Set the sauté pan over medium heat. Pour the oil into the sauté pan and let the oil heat for 1 minute.

✳ Using the tongs or spatula, put the fish sticks into the pan, one by one. The coating should sizzle when it touches the oil.

5 cook the fish sticks

* Put as many fish sticks in the pan as will fit without crowding. There should be a little space around each stick.

* Cook the fish sticks until golden brown on the first side, about 5 minutes.

* Using the tongs or spatula, carefully turn the fish sticks over. Cook the fish sticks on the second side until they are golden, about 5 minutes more.

6 keep warm

* Transfer the fish sticks onto the paper towels to drain.

* Turn the oven to 200°F. Place the first batch of fish sticks in the baking dish. Slide the dish into the oven to keep the fish sticks warm.

* Repeat steps 5 and 6 to cook the rest of the fish sticks.

7 serve it up

* Ask an adult to help you remove the fish sticks from the oven.

* Use the tongs to transfer the fish sticks to a platter.

* Serve the fish sticks hot, with lemon wedges for squeezing and tartar sauce or ketchup for dipping.

spaghetti & meatballs

ingredients

garlic 1 clove

olive oil 1 tablespoon

chopped tomatoes 1 can (28 ounces)

salt 4 teaspoons

oregano 1 tablespoon

tomato paste 3 tablespoons

water 1 cup

ground beef 1 pound

large egg 1

saltine crackers 6, crushed

ground pepper ¼ teaspoon

spaghetti 1 pound

grated Parmesan cheese for serving

tools

measuring cups & spoons

can opener

cutting board & sharp knife

metal spatula

large sauté pan with lid

oven mitts

wooden spoon

large bowl

plate

tongs

large pot

long-handled wooden fork

colander

1 chop the garlic

✳ Before you start, be sure an adult is nearby to help.

✳ Put the garlic clove on the cutting board. Place the flat part of the metal spatula on top of the garlic clove and press down hard with the heel of your palm to break and loosen the papery skin. Don't worry if you smash the garlic a little.

✳ Peel off the skin and throw it away. Use the knife to cut the garlic into little pieces.

2 cook the garlic

✳ Get an adult to help you now. Place the sauté pan over medium heat. Pour the olive oil into the sauté pan and let it heat for 1 minute.

✳ Add the garlic and stir with the wooden spoon until you can really smell it, about 30 seconds. Don't let it burn!

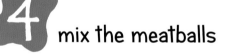

3 make the sauce

✹ Add the tomatoes, 1 teaspoon of the salt, 1½ teaspoons of the oregano, 2 tablespoons of the tomato paste, and the 1 cup water to the sauté pan. Stir with the wooden spoon until small bubbles appear on the surface of the sauce. This is called a simmer.

✹ Partially cover the pan with the lid and reduce the heat to low. Let the sauce simmer gently, stirring occasionally, for 15 minutes while you make the meatballs. You will have about 4 cups sauce.

4 mix the meatballs

✹ In the bowl, combine the ground beef, egg, crushed saltine crackers, 1 teaspoon of the salt, the remaining 1½ teaspoons of the oregano, the pepper, and the remaining 1 tablespoon tomato paste.

✹ Wash and dry your hands thoroughly. Mix and squeeze the mixture with your hands until it is smooth. (Or, you can use the wooden spoon to mix.)

5 shape the meatballs

✹ Still using your hands, pluck or scoop a rounded tablespoon of meat from the bowl and roll it between your palms to make a small meatball. Repeat, shaping about 20 small meatballs in all. As you make the meatballs, set them on the plate.

✹ Wash your hands well before continuing with the recipe.

6 cook the meatballs

✱ Turn up the heat under the tomato sauce to medium. Using the tongs, carefully put the meatballs into the sauce and cook them gently until they are cooked through, about 10 minutes.

✱ To test whether the meatballs are done, use the tongs to remove one, put it on the cutting board, and break it in half. It should be the same grayish color throughout.

✱ When the meatballs are done, remove the sauté pan from the heat. Cover to keep warm and set aside.

7 cook the spaghetti

✱ Fill the large pot three-quarters full with water. Place over high heat and bring to a rolling boil. When the water is boiling, add the remaining 2 teaspoons salt.

✱ Add the spaghetti to the pot, wait a minute, then stir and push the spaghetti down into the water with the wooden fork.

✱ Boil the spaghetti, stirring occasionally to keep it from clumping, until tender but not mushy, about 10 minutes, or according to the directions on the package.

8 put it all together

✱ Set the colander in the sink. Ask an adult to help you pour the spaghetti into the colander. Let the spaghetti drain, shaking the colander a few times to shake off the extra water.

✱ Add the drained spaghetti to the sauce in the sauté pan. Toss until it is well coated with the sauce.

✱ Using the tongs, divide the spaghetti among 4 plates. Add the meatballs, dividing them evenly, then spoon some extra sauce onto each plate of spaghetti. Pass the grated Parmesan cheese at the table.

after-school snacks

guacamole & chips

ingredients

green onions 2

ripe tomato 1

ripe avocados 3

limes 2

salt ½ teaspoon

cumin ½ teaspoon (optional)

cayenne pepper 1 pinch (optional)

fresh cilantro 5 or 6 sprigs

tortilla chips for serving

tools

measuring spoons

cutting board

sharp knife

medium bowl

small bowl

large spoon

citrus juicer

potato masher

plastic wrap (optional)

1 chop the green onions

✶ Before you start, be sure an adult is nearby to help.

✶ Put the green onions on the cutting board. Using the knife, cut off the root ends and several inches of the dark green tops. Slice each green onion in half lengthwise. Gather the pieces tightly together and chop finely crosswise.

✶ Put the onions into the medium bowl.

2 seed the tomato

✶ Put the tomato on the cutting board. Using the knife, cut across the top of the tomato to remove any stem or leaves. Insert the tip of the knife in the top and turn the blade in a circle, removing the tough core.

✶ Put the tomato on its side on the cutting board. Using the sharp knife, cut the tomato in half crosswise.

✶ Holding a tomato half over the small bowl or the sink, use the spoon to scoop out the seeds. Repeat with the other half. Discard the seeds.

why are my avocados turning brown after being cut?

* This is called oxidation and it happens when the cut surfaces meet with the oxygen in the air. Apples, pears, and artichokes do the same thing. Adding an acid, such as lime juice, helps prevent oxidation from happening. If you need to refrigerate your guacamole before serving it, press a piece of plastic wrap directly onto the surface of the guacamole. This will also help keep air from reacting with the surface of the guacamole and turning it brown.

3 dice the tomato

* Place the tomato halves on the cutting board and cut each half into 5 strips.

* A few at a time, gather the strips into a bundle and cut them crosswise to form small, even cubes. Add the tomatoes to the green onions in the bowl.

4 peel the avocados

* Ask an adult to help you cut the avocados in half lengthwise around the large pits in the centers. Twist in opposite directions to separate the halves.

* Using the spoon, scoop the avocado flesh out of each half into the bowl. Throw away the pits and the skins.

* Put the limes on the cutting board. Cut them in half crosswise with the knife. Twist each lime half over the cone of the citrus juicer to juice them.

7 add the cilantro

* Just before serving, strip the cilantro leaves from the stems and place on the cutting board.

* Holding the sharp knife in one hand and placing the fingers of your other hand on top of the knife, rock the knife back and forth over the cilantro leaves until they are cut into small, even pieces. You should have about 2 tablespoons chopped cilantro.

* Stir the chopped cilantro into the guacamole until incorporated.

* Serve with tortilla chips for dipping.

5 mash it together

* Stir in three-fourths of the lime juice and the salt. If you want a little smoky flavor, add the cumin. If you like your dip a little spicy, add the cayenne.

* Use the potato masher to mash everything together into a chunky paste.

6 season the dip

* Taste the guacamole and add more salt or lime juice if you want.

* If you are serving it later, press a piece of plastic wrap directly onto the surface of the guacamole and put it in the refrigerator.

deviled eggs

ingredients

large eggs 4
mayonnaise 2 tablespoons
Dijon mustard ½ teaspoon
salt
ground pepper
paprika 8 small pinches

tools

measuring spoons
saucepan
cutting board & sharp knife
soup spoon
medium bowl

1 cook the eggs

✳ Before you start, be sure an adult is nearby to help.

✳ Put the eggs in the saucepan and fill half full with water. Set over medium heat. When the water bubbles gently, reduce the heat to low and cook for 15 minutes.

2 let the eggs cool

✳ Ask an adult to help you remove the saucepan from the heat and place it in the sink. Run cold water over the eggs until both the water and the pan feel cool. Let the eggs cool in the water for 10 minutes.

✳ When the eggs are cool enough to handle, take them out of the water. Roll each egg on the work surface to crack the shell. Carefully peel off the eggshell.

3 flavor the yolks

✳ Put the eggs on the cutting board. Using the knife, cut each egg in half lengthwise. Use the spoon to scoop the yolks out of the eggs and into the bowl. Put the egg white halves on a serving platter and set aside.

✳ Add the mayonnaise and mustard to the bowl with the yolks. Use the spoon to mash them all together into a paste. Taste and season with salt and pepper.

4 mound the yolks

✳ Carefully spoon a small mound of the yolk mixture back into each egg white half.

✳ For each stuffed egg half, pick up a pinch of paprika and sprinkle it on the yellow part. Serve right away.

more ideas!

deviled eggs with pickles

Follow the recipe for Deviled Eggs but omit the paprika. In step 3, add 1 tablespoon finely chopped sweet pickle to the egg yolks. Proceed with the recipe to flavor the yolk mixture, mound it into the whites, and serve.

curried deviled eggs

Follow the recipe for Deviled Eggs but omit the paprika. In step 3, add ½ teaspoon curry powder to the egg yolks. Proceed with the recipe to flavor the yolks and mound them into the whites. Decorate the top of the stuffed eggs with chopped fresh parsley and serve.

deviled egg sandwiches

Follow steps 1 and 2 of the recipe for
Deviled Eggs to cook and peel the eggs.
Chop the whole eggs into ¼-inch pieces.
Mix the chopped eggs with the mayonnaise,
mustard, salt, and pepper. Spread slices of
small cocktail rye bread with the chopped
egg mixture, and top with slices of green or
black olive, if you like. Serve open faced
or topped with another slice of rye bread.

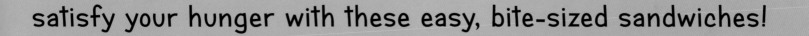

satisfy your hunger with these easy, bite-sized sandwiches!

strawberry smoothie

ingredients

fresh or frozen strawberries 6

ice 6 cubes

orange juice 1 cup

banana 1, peeled and cut
into chunks

plain, vanilla, or berry yogurt ½ cup

tools

measuring cups

cutting board

paring knife

blender

2 tall glasses

2 straws

1 trim the berries

✳ Before you start, be sure an adult is
nearby to help.

✳ Using the paring knife, cut a thick slice
from the top of each berry to remove the
stem. (If you are using frozen strawberries,
you can skip this step.)

2 blend it all together

✳ Put the strawberries, ice, orange juice,
banana, and yogurt into the blender container.
Cover the blender with the lid and hold down
the lid while you blend. Blend on high speed
until the mixture is frothy and there are no
big chunks of fruit or ice, 30–40 seconds.

✳ Pour the smoothie into 2 glasses. Serve
right away with straws.

more ideas!

peach smoothie

Follow the recipe for Strawberry Smoothie but replace the strawberries and orange juice with ½ cup fresh or frozen peach chunks and 1 cup apple juice. Add ¼ teaspoon ground cinnamon before you blend everything together.

pineapple smoothie

Follow the recipe for Strawberry Smoothie but replace the strawberries and orange juice with ½ cup fresh or canned pineapple chunks and 1 cup pineapple juice.

purple cow

Follow the recipe for Strawberry Smoothie but replace the strawberries and orange juice with ½ cup fresh or frozen blueberries and 1 cup purple grape juice.

share one with friends and see whose tongue turns purplest!

hummus

ingredients

garlic 1 clove

chickpeas (garbanzo beans)
1 can (15 ounces), rinsed
and drained

salt 1 teaspoon

water 1/3 cup

tahini (sesame paste) 1/3 cup

olive oil 1 tablespoon

juice of 2 lemons

pita bread 2 rounds

baby carrots 1/2 pound

tools

measuring cups & spoons

can opener

citrus juicer

cutting board

sharp knife

metal spatula

blender

rubber spatula

serrated knife

plastic wrap (optional)

1 slice the garlic

✻ Before you start, be sure an adult is nearby to help. Put the garlic clove on the cutting board. Place the metal spatula over the garlic clove and press down hard with the heel of your palm to loosen the papery skin. Peel off the skin and throw it away. Use the knife to cut the garlic into 4 or 5 slices.

2 blend the ingredients

✻ Put the garlic, chickpeas, salt, and water in the blender container. Blend for 1 minute. Turn off the blender and scrape down the sides with the rubber spatula. Replace the lid and blend again until the mixture is smooth, about 1 minute. Add the tahini, olive oil, and lemon juice and blend for another minute to mix.

3 scrape into a bowl

✻ Using the rubber spatula, scrape the hummus into a serving bowl. If you are not serving it immediately, cover the bowl with plastic wrap and refrigerate it.

4 serve the dip

✻ Place the pita bread rounds on the cutting board and use the serrated knife to cut each round into 8 triangles.

✻ Trim the stringy ends from the carrots. You can leave on the green tops, if you want, because they make a good handle.

✻ Put the bowl of hummus on a large plate. Surround it with the pita triangles and baby carrots for dipping.

oodles of noodles

pad thai

ingredients

**dried flat rice noodles
(¼ inch wide)** 1 package (7 ounces)

**fresh cilantro, basil, and/or mint
leaves** 10–12 sprigs

unsalted roasted peanuts
2 tablespoons

garlic 3 cloves

vegetable oil 2 tablespoons

cooked small (bay) shrimp 1 cup

sugar 1 tablespoon

Thai fish sauce 3 tablespoons

tomato ketchup 1½ tablespoons

large eggs 2, lightly beaten

bean sprouts 1 cup

lime 1, cut into wedges

tools

measuring cups & spoons

large saucepan

wooden spoon

cutting board

sharp knife

3 small bowls

metal spatula

colander

large sauté pan

1 soak the noodles

✳ Before you start, be sure an adult is nearby to help.

✳ Fill the saucepan three-quarters full of water. Set over high heat and bring to a rolling boil.

✳ Ask an adult to help you remove the saucepan from the heat. Drop the noodles into the saucepan and stir well with the wooden spoon. Let the noodles soak in the water until tender, about 30 minutes. Meanwhile, make the sauce.

2 chop herbs & nuts

✳ Strip the leaves from the cilantro or other herb sprigs and place the leaves on the cutting board.

✳ Using the knife, chop the leaves coarsely. You should have 3 tablespoons. Put the chopped leaves in one of the small bowls and set aside.

✳ Put the peanuts on the cutting board and use the knife to chop them coarsely. Put the chopped peanuts in another small bowl and set aside.

3 chop the garlic

✳ Put the garlic cloves on the cutting board. Place the flat side of the metal spatula over 1 garlic clove and press down hard with the heel of your palm to loosen the papery skin. Peel off the skin and throw it away. Repeat with the other 2 cloves. Use the knife to chop the garlic cloves into small pieces. Put the garlic in the third small bowl.

✳ Place the colander in the sink. When the noodles are tender, ask an adult to help you pour them into the colander.

4 cook garlic & shrimp

✳ Make sure all your ingredients are lined up and ready to go. From this point on, you'll be cooking fast!

✳ Get an adult to help you now. Set the sauté pan over medium heat. Pour the oil into the pan. Heat the oil for 1 minute.

✳ Toss the garlic into the sauté pan and fry, stirring with the wooden spoon, until golden, about 30 seconds.

✳ Add the shrimp to the sauté pan and cook, stirring with the wooden spoon, for 30 seconds.

5 add the seasonings

✳ Add the sugar, fish sauce, and ketchup to the sauté pan and cook, stirring, until the sugar dissolves, 10–15 seconds. (The fish sauce will smell a little stinky, but don't worry. Mixed with the other ingredients and cooked a little, it will help your pad Thai taste the same as it does when your order it from a Thai restaurant.)

6 cook the eggs

* Pour the beaten eggs into the sauté pan. Cook the eggs without stirring until they are barely set, about 30 seconds.

* Then stir the eggs well to scramble them and mix the eggs with the other ingredients in the pan.

7 add the noodles

* Add the drained noodles to the sauté pan and cook, stirring, for 2 minutes.

* Toss in three-fourths of the bean sprouts and cook, stirring, until the sprouts are just heated through, 1–2 minutes.

8 serve it up

* Ask an adult to help you remove the sauté pan from the heat and pour the contents onto a serving platter.

* Sprinkle with the remaining bean sprouts, the chopped peanuts, and the chopped herbs.

* Serve right away with the lime wedges on the side for squeezing.

parmesan pasta

ingredients

salt 2 teaspoons

farfalle (bow tie) pasta ¾ pound

frozen peas 1 cup

heavy cream 1½ cups

cooked ham 1½ cups diced

fresh herbs such as parsley, basil, chives, and oregano ½ cup leaves, finely chopped

Parmesan cheese ¼ cup grated, plus more for serving

tools

measuring cups & spoons

cutting board

sharp knife

box grater-shredder

large saucepan or pot

oven mitts

long-handled wooden fork

colander

large sauté pan

wooden spoon

tongs

1 boil the water

✱ Before you start, be sure an adult is nearby to help.

✱ Fill the saucepan three-quarters full with water. Place over high heat and bring to a rolling boil. Add the salt.

2 cook the pasta

✱ Add the pasta to the saucepan. Wait a minute, then stir and push the pasta down into the water with the wooden fork. Boil, stirring occasionally, until the pasta is tender but not mushy, about 12 minutes, or according to the directions on the package. When 11 minutes have past, add the peas.

✱ Set the colander in the sink. Ask an adult to help you pour the pasta and peas into the colander. Let drain.

3 warm the cream

✱ Put the cream and ham in the sauté pan. Set over medium heat and stir occasionally with the wooden spoon.

✱ When the cream is just beginning to bubble a little bit around the edge of the pan, add the herbs and drained pasta. Stir everything together with the wooden spoon.

4 stir in the cheese

✱ As soon as the pasta is heated through, after 1–2 minutes, ask an adult to help you remove the sauté pan from the heat.

✱ Stir in the ¼ cup Parmesan cheese. Use tongs to divide the pasta among bowls or plates. Serve hot.

✱ Pass more grated cheese at the table.

garlic & herb angel hair

makes
4-6
servings

ingredients

garlic 8 cloves

fresh parsley 8 sprigs

olive oil 3 tablespoons

red pepper flakes ¼ teaspoon
(optional)

salt 2 teaspoons

angel hair (capellini) pasta ¾ pound

lemon zest 1½ teaspoons grated

ground pepper

grated Parmesan cheese
for serving

tools

measuring cups & spoons

box grater-shredder

cutting board & sharp knife

metal spatula

large sauté pan

wooden spoon

large saucepan or pot

oven mitts

long-handled wooden fork

colander

ladle

tongs

1 peel the garlic

✳ Before you start, be sure an adult is
nearby to help.

✳ Put the garlic cloves on the cutting
board. Place the flat part of the metal
spatula over 1 garlic clove and press down
hard with the heel of your palm to break
and loosen the papery skin. Don't worry
if you smash the garlic a little. Peel off the
skin and throw it away. Repeat with the
other 7 cloves.

2 chop garlic & herbs

✳ Use the knife to slice the garlic cloves
thinly crosswise.

✳ Strip the parsley leaves off the stems
and place them on the cutting board.

✳ Holding the sharp knife in one hand and
placing the fingers of your other hand on top
of the knife, rock the knife back and forth
over the parsley leaves until they are cut
into small, even pieces.

* Garlic can easily burn and turn bitter if you cook it over too high heat without stirring.

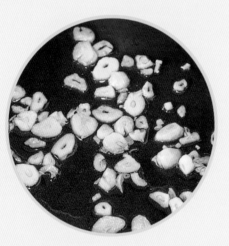

* Cook the garlic over low to medium-low heat and keep a close eye on it. If you can smell it, you know the garlic is almost done.

avoided!

3 cook the garlic

* Get an adult to help you now. Set the sauté pan over medium-low heat and pour the oil into the pan. Heat the oil for 1 minute.

* Add the sliced garlic and red pepper flakes (if you like your pasta spicy) and cook, stirring frequently with the wooden spoon, until the garlic is just beginning to turn golden, 3–4 minutes. Remove the sauté pan from the heat.

4 cook the pasta

* Fill the saucepan three-quarters full with water. Place the pan over high heat and bring to a rolling boil.

* When the water is boiling, add the salt.

* Add the pasta to the saucepan, wait a minute, then stir and push the pasta down into the water with the wooden fork. Boil, stirring occasionally, until the pasta is tender but not mushy, about 6 minutes, or according to the directions on the package.

5 drain the pasta

✻ Set the colander in the sink.

✻ Ask an adult to help you now. Ladle out 1 cup of the pasta cooking water and set it aside in a liquid measuring cup.

✻ Ask an adult to help you pour the pasta into the colander. Let the pasta drain.

6 cook the flavorings

✻ Place the sauté pan back over medium heat and add the lemon zest and parsley. Stir with the wooden spoon to combine the ingredients.

7 toss it all together

✻ Add the pasta and ½ cup of the pasta cooking water to the sauté pan. Toss the ingredients together with the tongs until combined, adding more of the reserved pasta water if the pasta seems dry.

✻ Taste (careful, it's hot!) and add pepper and more salt if needed.

✻ Serve right away. Pass the grated Parmesan cheese at the table.

more ideas!

smoked salmon angel hair

In a large sauté pan over medium-low heat, cook 8 cloves garlic, thinly sliced, in 2 tablespoons olive oil until just golden, 3–4 minutes. Add ⅔ cup heavy cream and 2 tablespoons chopped fresh dill and cook, stirring, until thickened, about 2 minutes. Add ½ pound smoked salmon, cut into ¾-inch pieces, and the grated zest and juice from 1 lemon. Cook and drain ¾ pound angel hair, then toss it with the salmon mixture. Serve right away.

shrimp & lemon angel hair

Follow the recipe for Garlic & Herb Angel Hair but add ½ pound peeled shrimp and 1 halved lemon, for squeezing. In step 3, before you add the garlic to the sauté pan, add the shrimp and cook, stirring, until they are firm and pink, 2–3 minutes. With a slotted spoon, remove the shrimp from the pan. Add the garlic and continue with the recipe. In step 7, add the shrimp to the pan with the pasta. Squeeze the lemon over just before serving.

tomato & salami angel hair

Follow the recipe for Garlic & Herb Angel Hair but add 1 cup small cherry tomatoes, cut in half, and ¼ pound thinly sliced salami, cut into small strips. Follow steps 1 and 2 of the recipe. In step 3, when the garlic is beginning to turn golden, add the cherry tomatoes and cook until they are just softened and juicy, 1–2 minutes. Continue with the recipe. In step 7, add the salami strips to the sauté pan with the pasta.

toss any of your favorite things into a bowl of hot pasta!

lasagna

ingredients

mozzarella cheese 1 pound

olive oil 1 tablespoon

ground turkey ½ pound

fresh turkey or chicken Italian-style sausages ¼ pound

tomato sauce 4 cans (15 ounces each)

lasagna noodles 9 (about 7 ounces)

salt 2 teaspoons

ricotta cheese 2 tubs (15 ounces each)

grated Parmesan cheese 1 cup

large eggs 2

tools

measuring cups & spoons

can opener

box grater-shredder & plate

large sauté pan

wooden spoon

large pot

long-handled wooden fork

large and small bowls

colander

9-by-13-by-2-inch baking dish

rubber spatula

oven mitts & cooling rack

aluminum foil

metal spatula

1 shred the cheese

✳ Before you start, be sure an adult is nearby to help.

✳ Hold the box grater-shredder on the plate with one hand. Holding the cheese in your other hand, rub the mozzarella over the large shredding holes of the box grater-shredder. Be careful not to scrape your fingers or knuckles on the holes!

2 cook the meat

✳ Ask an adult to help you now. Put the olive oil in the sauté pan and set it over medium heat. Add the ground turkey. Using the wooden spoon, break up any large chunks. Squeeze the sausages from their casings. Add the sausage meat to the sauté pan.

✳ With the wooden spoon, keep pushing the ground turkey and the sausage around in the sauté pan until they are no longer pink. This will take about 5 minutes.

3 simmer the sauce

* Add the tomato sauce to the sauté pan and stir to coat the meat. Heat the mixture until small bubbles start to form in the tomato sauce; this is called a simmer.

* Simmer the sauce, stirring occasionally, for 10–12 minutes. Remove from the heat and set aside.

4 cook the pasta

* Fill the large pot three-quarters full with water. Place over high heat and bring to a rolling boil.

* When the water is boiling, add the salt.

* Drop in the noodles, then push them down into the water with the wooden fork. Boil the noodles, stirring occasionally, until flexible but still a little chewy, 7–8 minutes, or according to the directions on the package of noodles.

5 make the filling

* While the pasta is cooking, you'll have time to make the cheese filling: In the large bowl, combine the ricotta cheese and ²/₃ cup of the Parmesan cheese.

* One at a time, crack the eggs into the small bowl and check for shells. Then pour the eggs into the bowl with the cheeses. Using the wooden spoon, beat until smooth.

* Set the colander in the sink. Ask an adult to help you pour the noodles into the colander. Rinse with cold water and drain again.

6 start to layer

✳ Position an oven rack in the center of the oven. Preheat the oven to 350°F.

✳ Put the baking dish on the counter in front of you. Arrange the tomato sauce, drained lasagna noodles, ricotta mixture, mozzarella cheese, and the remaining ⅓ cup Parmesan cheese next to you.

✳ Use the rubber spatula to spread ½ cup of the tomato sauce in the bottom of the baking dish. Lay 3 lasagna noodles, side by side, over the sauce. Spread half of the ricotta over the noodles. Top with one-third of the mozzarella. Spread 2 cups tomato sauce over the cheese.

7 finish layering

✳ Repeat the layering, adding 3 more noodles, the rest of the ricotta, half of the remaining mozzarella cheese, and another 2 cups tomato sauce on top.

✳ Top with the final 3 noodles, the last 2 cups tomato sauce, and the rest of the mozzarella cheese.

✳ Sprinkle the finished lasagna with the remaining Parmesan. Cover the baking dish with aluminum foil.

8 bake, cool & serve

✳ Put the baking dish in the oven and bake for 30 minutes. Ask an adult to help you remove the foil. Bake uncovered until the cheese is lightly golden and the lasagna is bubbling around the edges, about 30 minutes longer.

✳ Ask an adult to help you take the dish out of the oven. Set the lasagna on the cooling rack and cool for 5–10 minutes. Using the metal spatula, cut down through the pasta layers to make 8 or 10 squares. Lift each square onto a plate to serve.

oodles of noodles **67**

put on your oven mitts

fish in a paper packet

ingredients

olive oil as needed

green onions 4

cherry tomatoes 12

fresh basil 2 sprigs

fish fillets such as flounder, sole, or red snapper 4 (5–6 ounces each)

sliced black olives ¼ cup, sliced (optional)

salt

ground pepper

lemon wedges for serving

tools

4 rectangles parchment paper (20 by 15 inches each)

cutting board

sharp knife

small serrated knife

baking sheet

oven mitts

scissors

1 before you start

✳ Be sure an adult is nearby to help.

✳ Position an oven rack in the center of the oven. Preheat the oven to 375°F.

✳ Place the parchment paper rectangles on a work surface. Using your fingers, lightly rub 1 side of each rectangle with olive oil.

2 slice the green onions

✳ Put the green onions on the cutting board. Using the sharp knife, cut off the root ends and several inches of the green tops.

✳ Slice the white parts and tender green parts in half lengthwise.

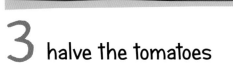

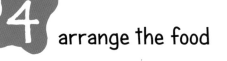

3 halve the tomatoes

✳ Using the serrated knife, cut the cherry tomatoes in half.

✳ Strip the basil leaves off the stems. You should have 8–12 leaves.

4 arrange the food

✳ Lay a piece of parchment paper in front of you. Crisscross 2 pieces of green onion on the parchment.

✳ Lay a piece of fish on top. Place 2 or 3 basil leaves over the fish. Add 6 cherry tomato halves, cut sides down, and a few olive slices, if using.

✳ Drizzle a little olive oil over the fish. Sprinkle with a little salt and pepper.

5 fold the paper

✳ To seal the packet, pull up the long edges of the parchment rectangle and make a tight fold at the top, creasing the parchment with your thumbnails.

✳ Fold down several times, as if you were folding down the top of a paper bag.

6 twist the ends

* One at a time, twist the ends of the paper several times to make a tight seal. The finished packet will look like a piece of wrapped candy.

* Fold the ends so that they stick upward. This way the fish juices won't run out of the packets while they are cooking.

* Repeat steps 4–6 to make the remaining packets.

7 bake the packets

* Put the fish packets onto the baking sheet. Slide the baking sheet into the oven.

* Bake the packets for 15 minutes.

8 serve the packets

* Ask an adult to help you remove the baking sheet from the oven. Holding the packets by the ends (careful, the middles are hot!), place each packet on a plate.

* Using the scissors, snip the ends of the packets on both sides.

* Serve right away with lemon wedges for squeezing. Tell your guests to watch out for the hot steam when they use their forks and knives to pull open the packets!

rosemary roast chicken

makes
4-6
servings

ingredients

lemon 1, juiced

olive oil ¼ cup

whole-grain Dijon mustard
3 tablespoons (optional)

bone-in chicken breast halves 2

chicken legs (drumsticks) 2

bone-in chicken thighs 2

fresh rosemary 2 tablespoons
chopped

salt ¼ teaspoon

pepper 1 pinch

tools

measuring cups & spoons

cutting board & paring knife

citrus juicer

9-by-13-by-2-inch baking dish

plastic wrap

oven mitts

tongs

large spoon

1 marinate the chicken

✳ Before you start, be sure an adult is nearby to help. Pour the lemon juice, olive oil, and mustard into the baking dish.

✳ Add the chicken pieces and coat them with the marinade. Sprinkle with the rosemary, salt, and pepper. Cover the dish and refrigerate for 1 hour, turning the chicken pieces once.

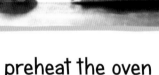

2 preheat the oven

✳ Remove the baking dish from the refrigerator and uncover. Turn the chicken pieces skin side up. Let the chicken stand at room temperature for 30 minutes.

✳ After 15 minutes of standing, position an oven rack in the center of the oven. Preheat the oven to 400°F.

3 roast the chicken

✳ Put the baking dish in the oven and roast the chicken until the skin is browned and the chicken is cooked through, about 50 minutes.

✳ Ask an adult to help you remove the dish from the oven.

4 serve it up

✳ To test the chicken for doneness, slide the tip of the paring knife into the thickest part of a drumstick. The juices should run clear or yellowish; if they are still pink, cook for another 5–10 minutes.

✳ Using the tongs, transfer the chicken pieces to a platter. Spoon a little of the cooking juices over each piece. Serve right away.

cheese pizza

ingredients

warm tap water 1 cup

dry yeast 1 package

cornmeal 4–5 tablespoons

olive oil 4½ tablespoons

salt 1 teaspoon, plus extra for sprinkling

all-purpose flour 2½ cups, plus extra for kneading

mozzarella cheese 4 cups shredded

large tomatoes 4, cored and thinly sliced

Parmesan cheese 2 tablespoons grated

ground pepper

fresh basil leaves 16–20

tools

measuring cups & spoons

box grater-shredder

cutting board & sharp knife

instant-read thermometer

large bowl

wooden spoon

plastic wrap

2 baking sheets

rolling pin

oven mitts

metal spatula

pizza cutter

1 start the dough

✱ Before you start, be sure an adult is nearby to help.

✱ The warm water must be between 115°F and 125°F. Use the thermometer to check the temperature. Pour the water into the large bowl. Sprinkle the yeast over the water and let stand until the yeast becomes foamy, about 5 minutes.

✱ Add 3 tablespoons of the cornmeal, 2 tablespoons of the olive oil, 1 teaspoon salt, and ½ cup of the flour to the bowl with the yeast.

2 mix the dough

✱ Using the wooden spoon, beat until the mixture is smooth.

✱ Add the remaining flour, ½ cup at a time, beating after each addition, until a soft dough forms. You might not need to add every bit of the flour.

✱ Sprinkle a work surface lightly with a little flour. Tip the dough out of the bowl onto the surface and get ready to knead.

3 knead the dough

✳ Dust your hands with flour. Using the heel of one hand, push the top half of the dough away from you. Then, fold the top half of the dough back toward you. Rotate the dough a quarter turn.

✳ Repeat these same movements, continuing to push, fold, and rotate the dough until it feels smooth and springy, about 10 minutes. While you knead, occasionally dust the work surface with flour to prevent sticking. Gather the dough into a ball.

4 let the dough rise

✳ Wash the large bowl and oil it lightly with ½ tablespoon of the olive oil.

✳ Put the dough in the bowl, flip it around in the bowl to coat it with the oil, and cover the bowl with plastic wrap.

✳ Note where the top of the dough is on the bowl. You can even mark it on the outside with a piece of tape if you like.

✳ Set the bowl in a warm place and let the dough rise until it has doubled in size, 45–60 minutes.

5 get ready to bake

✳ Place an oven rack as low as possible in the oven. Preheat the oven to 450°F.

✳ Sprinkle the baking sheets with the remaining 1–2 tablespoons cornmeal, coating the surface evenly.

6 smack the dough

✳ Wipe off your work surface and dust it with a little flour.

✳ Sink your fist into the risen dough to deflate it and then gather the dough into a ball. Tip the dough out of the bowl onto the work surface.

✳ Using the rolling pin, smack the dough firmly all over 4 or 5 times. Rotate the dough a half turn and smack it again 4 or 5 times. Flip the dough over and repeat. (Smacking the dough will make it easier to work with.) Divide the dough in half.

7 shape the pizza rounds

✳ Using your hands, roll, press, and stretch one half of the dough into a 12-inch circle. Slide your hands under the round and lift it onto a prepared baking sheet. Pinch up the outer edge to make a ridge.

✳ Using your fingers, rub 1 tablespoon of the oil all over the dough round. Sprinkle half of the mozzarella over the pizza. Top it with half of the tomato slices and sprinkle with 1 tablespoon of the grated Parmesan cheese, some salt and pepper, and a few fresh basil leaves.

8 bake the pizza

✳ Slide the baking pan into the oven and bake until the crust is browned and the cheese is bubbling, about 15 minutes. While the first pizza is baking, shape the second pizza dough round, place it on the other baking sheet, and add the toppings.

✳ Ask an adult to help you remove the first pizza from the oven. Then, put the second pizza in the oven to bake.

✳ Using the metal spatula, slide the first pizza onto the cutting board. Using the pizza cutter, cut into wedges and serve.

more ideas!

pineapple & ham pizza

Follow the recipe for Cheese Pizza but reduce the olive oil to 2½ tablespoons. In step 7, use a spoon to spread 1 cup tomato sauce or pasta sauce over the dough round instead of the olive oil. Replace the tomato slices and basil leaves with 1 cup each ham strips and fresh or canned pineapple cut into ½-inch chunks. Bake the pizza as directed.

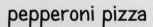

pepperoni pizza

Follow the recipe for Cheese Pizza but reduce the olive oil to 2½ tablespoons. In step 7, use a spoon to spread 1 cup tomato sauce or pasta sauce over the dough round instead of the olive oil. Replace the tomato slices and basil leaves with ¼ pound thinly sliced pepperoni. Bake the pizza as directed.

black olive pizza

Follow the recipe for Cheese Pizza but reduce the olive oil to 2½ tablespoons. In step 7, use a spoon to spread 1 cup tomato sauce or pasta sauce over the dough round instead of the olive oil. Replace the tomato slices and basil leaves with 1 cup thinly sliced black olives. Bake the pizza as directed.

turn your kitchen into a pizza parlor with your favorite toppings!

shepherd's pie

ingredients

baking potatoes 3 pounds
(6 or 7 potatoes)

salt

whole milk 1 cup

butter 2 tablespoons

ground pepper

carrots 2 peeled

onion 1

olive oil 1 tablespoon

ground lamb 1 pound

dried thyme ½ teaspoon

all-purpose flour 1 tablespoon

beef broth 1 cup

tomato paste 1 tablespoon

tools

measuring cups & spoons

vegetable peeler

cutting board & sharp knife

large & small saucepans

colander

oven mitts

potato masher

large sauté pan with lid

wooden spoon

9-inch baking dish

rubber spatula

1 boil the potatoes

✳ Before you start, be sure an adult is nearby to help. Peel the potatoes. Using the knife, cut each potato in half crosswise. Lay each half flat side down on the board and cut it in half again. Put the quartered potatoes in the large saucepan. Add enough water to cover the potatoes by 1 inch. Add 1 teaspoon salt.

✳ Cover the saucepan and place it over medium-high heat. Bring the water to a boil. Boil the potatoes until they are tender when pierced with the knife, about 15 minutes.

2 mash the potatoes

✳ Set the colander in the sink. Ask an adult to help you pour the potatoes into the colander. Let the potatoes drain.

✳ Pour the milk into the small saucepan and add the butter. Set the saucepan over low heat until the butter melts.

✳ Put the potatoes back into the large pan. Using the potato masher, start mashing, adding the milk mixture a little at a time. Keep mashing and adding milk until the potatoes are smooth and creamy. Season with salt and pepper, cover, and set aside.

3 dice the carrots

✳ One at a time, put the peeled carrots on the cutting board and, using the knife, cut off the stem end. Cut each carrot crosswise into 3 pieces.

✳ Cut each carrot piece in half lengthwise. Then, lay each piece flat side down and cut in half lengthwise again. You'll have 24 sticks in all.

✳ A few at a time, stack the sticks into a pile. Hold the stack of sticks together with one hand. With your other hand, cut the sticks crosswise into small cubes.

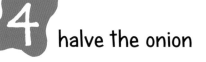 halve the onion

✳ Put the onion on the cutting board. Using the knife, cut the onion in half through the stem end and peel off the skin.

✳ Put an onion half flat side down on the cutting board. Use one hand to hold the onion at the stem end. With the knife tip pointed toward the stem end, cut ¼-inch slices. Do not cut through the stem end. (The uncut section helps keep the onion together as you cut.)

5 dice the onion

✳ Turn the knife blade so it is parallel to the cutting board. Cut the onion horizontally into ¼-inch slices. As before, do not cut through the stem end.

✳ Finally, cut the onion crosswise to make small cubes, or dice.

6 cook the vegetables

✳ Preheat the oven to 375°F.

✳ Get an adult to help you now. Set the sauté pan over medium heat. Pour the olive oil into the pan. Let the oil heat for 1 minute.

✳ Add the carrots and onion to the sauté pan. Cook, stirring frequently with the wooden spoon, until the carrots and onions are soft and the onions look clear instead of white, about 10 minutes.

7 cook the lamb

✳ Add the lamb and thyme to the sauté pan and cook, stirring with the wooden spoon to break up any large clumps, until the meat is no longer pink.

✳ Sprinkle the flour over the meat and cook, stirring, for 1 minute. Add the beef broth and tomato paste. Stir well.

✳ Turn the heat down to low, cover the sauté pan, and cook, stirring occasionally, until the mixture is slightly thickened and the flavors are blended, about 15 minutes.

8 assemble the pie

✳ Ask an adult to help you remove the sauté pan from the heat. Using the rubber spatula, scrape the lamb mixture into the baking dish and spread evenly.

✳ Use the rubber spatula to spread the mashed potatoes in a thick, even layer over the lamb mixture.

✳ Put the pie dish in the oven and bake until the lamb and potatoes are heated through and the top is turning golden. (If your mashed potatoes are freshly made and warm to start with, this should take about 15 minutes. If they are cold, it may take 25–30 minutes.) Serve right away.

glazed baby back ribs

ingredients

large lemon 1

tomato ketchup 1 cup

honey 2 tablespoons

Worcestershire sauce
1½ tablespoons

butter 1 tablespoon

ground ginger ¾ teaspoon

ground coriander ¾ teaspoon

garlic 1 large clove

baby back ribs 2 pounds (2 racks)

tools

measuring cups & spoons

large roasting pan

aluminum foil

cutting board & sharp knife

citrus juicer

small saucepan

metal spatula

wooden spoon

oven mitts

tongs

meat fork

1 before you start

✳ Be sure an adult is nearby to help.

✳ Position an oven rack in the center of
the oven. Preheat the oven to 350°F.

✳ Line the roasting pan with aluminum foil.

2 begin the glaze

✳ Put the lemon on the cutting board.
With the sharp knife, cut the lemon in half
crosswise. Twist the lemon halves over the
cone of the citrus juicer to juice it. Pick out
the seeds, measure out 3 tablespoons juice,
and then add it to the saucepan.

✳ Add the ketchup, honey, Worcestershire
sauce, butter, ginger, and ground coriander
to the saucepan.

3 chop the garlic

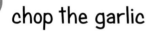

✳ Put the garlic clove on the cutting board. Place the flat part of the metal spatula over the garlic clove and press down hard with the heel of your palm to break and loosen the papery skin. Don't worry if you smash the garlic a little. Peel off the skin and throw it away.

✳ With the knife, chop the garlic into tiny pieces. Add the garlic pieces to the small saucepan.

4 boil the glaze

✳ Set the saucepan over medium heat and bring the ketchup mixture to a boil, stirring constantly with the wooden spoon. Turn off the heat.

5 coat & cook the ribs

✳ Put the ribs in the foil-lined roasting pan.

✳ Pour the glaze over the ribs, turning the ribs to coat both sides with the glaze. Arrange the ribs meaty side up.

✳ Cover the roasting pan tightly with another layer of aluminum foil, put it in the oven, and bake for 1 hour.

6 remove the ribs

✳ Ask an adult to help you open the oven and carefully slide out the oven rack. Wearing oven mitts, carefully lift the roasting pan from the oven and place it on a heatproof counter or other surface.

7 brown the ribs

✳ Using the tongs, carefully pull back the aluminum foil from the roasting pan. Be careful: the foil and steam will be very hot! Throw away the foil.

✳ Ask an adult to help you put the roasting pan with the ribs back in the oven. Bake the ribs until they are browned and the meat is very tender, about 1 hour longer.

✳ Ask an adult to help you remove the roasting pan from the oven.

8 separate the ribs

✳ To serve, let the ribs cool in the pan for 5–10 minutes. Using the tongs, transfer the racks to a cutting board.

✳ Ask an adult to help you now. Holding the ribs steady with the meat fork, use the knife to slice between the bones and separate the individual ribs.

✳ Pile the ribs onto a serving plate and serve right away.

don't forget the veggies

stuffed baked potatoes

ingredients

baking potatoes 4

frozen vegetables such as peas, carrots, corn, or broccoli, or a mix 1 cup

ham or smoked turkey 2 or 3 slices (optional)

sour cream ¼ cup

whole milk ¼ cup

Cheddar or Swiss cheese 1 cup shredded (¼ pound)

salt

pepper

tools

measuring cups

box grater-shredder

cutting board & sharp knife

oven mitts

spoon

medium bowl

cookie sheet

1 before you start

✳ Be sure an adult is nearby to help.

✳ Position an oven rack in the center of the oven. Preheat the oven to 350°F.

✳ Put the potatoes on the cutting board. Using the knife, make 2 deep slits, 1 lengthwise and 1 crosswise, across the top of each potato. Cut about halfway into the potato.

2 bake the potatoes

✳ Put the potatoes in the oven, directly on the oven rack, and bake until they feel soft when you squeeze them—wear your oven mitts!—about 1 hour.

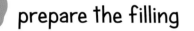

3 prepare the filling

✳ While the potatoes are baking, cook the frozen vegetables according to the directions on the package. Set them aside until they are cool enough to handle.

✳ Using the cutting board and the sharp knife, chop any of the large cooked vegetables (peas and corn kernels can stay whole) and the ham, if using, into tiny pieces. Set aside.

4 remove the potatoes

✳ When the potatoes are ready, ask an adult to help you remove them from the oven, but leave the oven on. Set the potatoes aside until they are cool enough to handle.

5 scoop out the flesh

✳ When you can handle the potatoes comfortably, use both hands to gently squeeze the potatoes so that the white, fluffy potato flesh starts to burst out from the skin.

✳ Using the spoon, scoop out the potato flesh, being careful not to poke through the skin on the bottom and sides. You should try to leave a wall of potato flesh about $1/4$ inch thick, so that the skin won't break when you try to stuff it.

✳ Put the potato flesh in the bowl. Set the skins aside.

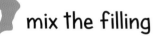

6 mix the filling

✻ Add the sour cream and milk to the bowl. Using the spoon, stir and mash the potato mixture until it is smooth.

✻ Stir in the cooked vegetables, ham (if you're using it), and $3/4$ cup of the shredded Cheddar or Swiss cheese.

✻ Taste and season with salt and pepper.

7 stuff the spuds

✻ Using the spoon, scoop the potato mixture back into the potato shells. Sprinkle each potato with a little of the remaining shredded cheese.

8 bake again

✻ Place the potatoes on the cookie sheet and put them back in the oven.

✻ Bake until the cheese is bubbly and the potatoes are heated through, about 15 minutes.

✻ Serve right away.

spring peas with mint

ingredients

fresh peas in the pod 2 pounds
or frozen peas 10 ounces
fresh mint 6 sprigs
butter 2 teaspoons
salt as needed

tools

measuring cups & spoons
medium bowl
cutting board & sharp knife
large saucepan or pot with lid
colander
wooden spoon

1 shell the peas

✱ Before you start, be sure an adult is nearby to help. If you are using fresh peas, snap off the stem ends and pull the "strings" down to the pointed ends to open the pods. Pop the peas out with your thumb into the bowl. (If you're using frozen peas, you can skip this step.)

2 slice the mint

✱ Strip the mint leaves from the stems. Throw away the stems and lay the leaves on the cutting board.

✱ Stack 4 or 5 leaves on top of one another, then roll up the stack lengthwise into a little tube. Using the knife, slice the tube into thin slices. Repeat until you have sliced all the leaves.

3 cook the peas

✱ Put about 1 inch of water in the saucepan. Place over high heat and bring to a boil. Add the fresh peas and cover. Turn the heat down to medium-high. Boil until the peas are just tender, 4–5 minutes. (If you're using frozen peas, follow the cooking directions on the package.)

4 toss it together

✱ Set the colander in the sink. Ask an adult to help you pour the peas into the colander. Let the peas drain well—shaking the colander helps—then pour them back into the empty saucepan.

✱ Add the butter, mint, and several pinches of salt to the saucepan. Stir until the butter melts. Serve right away.

roasted carrots

makes **4** servings

ingredients

carrots 1 pound

butter 1 tablespoon, cut into little pieces

brown sugar 2 tablespoons

ground ginger ¼ teaspoon

salt ½ teaspoon

ground pepper ¼ teaspoon

tools

measuring spoons

vegetable peeler

cutting board & sharp knife

9-by-13-by-2-inch baking dish

oven mitts

wooden spoon

1 before you start

✱ Be sure an adult is nearby to help.

✱ Position an oven rack in the center of the oven. Preheat the oven to 375°F.

2 slice the carrots

✱ Put the carrots on the cutting board. Using the knife, cut the tops off the carrots and discard them.

✱ Using the vegetable peeler, peel the carrots. Throw away the peels.

✱ Switch back to the knife and cut the carrots on the diagonal into slices about ½ inch thick.

3 roast the carrots

✱ Put the carrots in an even layer in the baking dish and dot with the butter.

✱ Put the baking dish in the oven and roast, stirring occasionally with the wooden spoon, until the carrots are tender and beginning to brown, about 35 minutes.

4 add some flavor

✱ Ask an adult to help you carefully remove the baking dish from the oven.

✱ Sprinkle the carrots with the brown sugar, ginger, salt, and pepper. Put the dish back in the oven and roast until the sugar is melted and syrupy, about 5 minutes.

✱ Ask an adult to help you take the dish out of the oven. Serve right away.

more ideas!

roasted potatoes

Cut 1 pound small (1½ inches in diameter) unpeeled red potatoes in half. Place them skin side down in in a 9-by-13-by-2-inch baking dish and dot with 1 tablespoon butter, cut into pieces. Roast the potatoes in a preheated 375°F oven until they are browned and tender, about 35 minutes. Season with salt and pepper.

roasted parsnips

Peel and trim 1½ pounds parsnips, then cut into ½-inch-thick diagonal slices. Arrange in a 9-by-13-by-2-inch baking dish and dot with 1 tablespoon butter, cut into pieces. Roast in a preheated 375°F oven until tender, about 30 minutes. Sprinkle the parsnips with the grated zest of 1 orange, 2 tablespoons brown sugar, ½ teaspoon allspice, ½ teaspoon salt, and ¼ teaspoon pepper and continue to roast for about 5 minutes.

roasted sweet potatoes

Follow the recipe for Roasted Carrots, but replace the carrots with 1½ pounds sweet potatoes. Scrub the sweet potatoes and peel them, if you wish (they're also good with the skins on). Put the sweet potatoes on the cutting board and ask an adult to help you cut them into 2-inch chunks. Place in the roasting pan, then roast and season as directed in the carrot recipe.

also called yams, sweet potatoes can be either yellow or orange

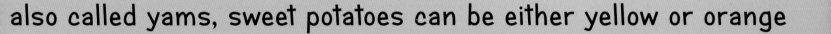

sautéed green beans

ingredients

shallots 4

salt 1 teaspoon, plus extra for seasoning

green beans 1 pound, stems snapped off

butter 1 tablespoon

balsamic vinegar 1 tablespoon

ground pepper

tools

measuring spoons

large saucepan

cutting board & sharp knife

colander

medium frying pan

wooden spoon

tongs

1 before you start

✳ Be sure an adult is nearby to help. Fill the saucepan half full with water. Place over high heat and bring to a boil.

✳ Cut off the stem ends of the shallots. Cut each shallot in half lengthwise. Peel off and throw away the papery outer skin. Slice the shallots thinly lengthwise.

2 cook the beans

✳ When the water is boiling, add the 1 teaspoon salt and drop in the beans.

✳ Boil the green beans until they are bright green and just tender, 3–5 minutes.

✳ Set the colander in the sink. Ask an adult to help you pour the beans into the colander. Rinse the beans with cold water until they are cool and drain again.

3 cook the shallots

✳ Put the butter in the frying pan over low heat and let it melt. When the butter foams, add the shallots and cook, stirring with the wooden spoon, until they are very soft and beginning to brown, 10–15 minutes.

✳ Add the vinegar and stir for another minute until the shallots are coated.

4 mix it together

✳ Add the drained beans to the frying pan. Raise the heat to medium and cook, tossing with the tongs, until the beans are heated through, about 1 minute.

✳ Taste and season with salt and pepper. Serve right away.

time for a sandwich

BLAT sandwich

ingredients

bacon 2 slices

ripe tomato 1

ripe avocado 1

sandwich bread 2 slices

mayonnaise 1–2 teaspoons

lettuce leaf 1

tools

measuring spoons

paper towels

2 plates

small frying pan

tongs

cutting board

small serrated knife

table knife

large spoon

toaster (optional)

large serrated (bread) knife

1 cook the bacon

✳ Before you start, be sure an adult is nearby to help.

✳ Put a few layers of paper towels on a plate. Put the bacon in the frying pan.

✳ Ask an adult to help you place the frying pan over low heat and fry the bacon until it is browned and crisp, 4–5 minutes. Use the tongs to turn the bacon over once or twice as it cooks so that both sides cook evenly.

2 drain the bacon

✳ Remove the frying pan from the heat. Using the tongs, put the bacon on the paper towels. (This will soak up all the extra fat from the bacon strips so your sandwich won't taste greasy.)

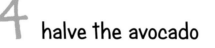

3 slice the tomato

✳ Put the tomato on the cutting board. Using the small serrated knife, cut across the top of the tomato to remove any stem or leaves. Insert the tip of the knife in the top and turn the blade in a circle, removing the tough core.

✳ Still using the serrated knife, cut the tomato crosswise into thin slices.

4 halve the avocado

✳ Place the avocado on the cutting board. Using the serrated knife, cut the avocado in half lengthwise.

✳ Twist the halves in opposite directions to separate them.

✳ Set aside the avocado half containing the pit to use for something else.

5 slice the avocado

✳ Hold the other avocado half in your palm. Using the table knife, cut down through the avocado flesh lengthwise, just to the skin, to make 5 or 6 slices.

✳ Use the spoon to scoop out the slices onto the cutting board. (The avocado is what turns a BLT into a BLAT.)

6 toast the bread

✳ Place the bread in the toaster and toast it until golden brown. (You can also use untoasted bread if you like it better, but toasting the bread helps prevent the sandwich from getting soggy.)

7 spread the bread

✳ Lay the toasted bread slices on the cutting board.

✳ Using the table knife, spread the mayonnaise over one (or both) of the toasted bread slices.

8 build the sandwich

✳ Arrange the avocado slices on top of the mayonnaise on 1 slice of toast.

✳ Cover the avocado with the bacon, tomato slices, and lettuce leaf.

✳ Top with the other slice of toast and press down gently.

✳ Using the large serrated knife, cut the sandwich in half. Serve right away.

turkey wrap

ingredients

English cucumber ⅓

lavash bread 1 sheet

cream cheese 1 tablespoon, at room temperature

fresh basil 4 leaves

turkey 2 or 3 slices

fresh spinach leaves 4

tools

measuring spoons

cutting board

sharp knife

table knife

1 slice the cucumber

✳ Before you start, be sure an adult is nearby to help.

✳ Put the cucumber on the cutting board. Using the sharp knife, cut off the ends. Slice the cucumber into rounds as thin as possible.

2 spread the bread

✳ Put the lavash bread on the cutting board. Using the sharp knife, trim the edges to make a neat, 8-inch square.

✳ Using the butter knife, spread the cream cheese over the lavash, leaving a 1-inch-wide border uncovered around the edges.

3 layer the fillings

✳ Layer the sliced cucumber on top of the cream cheese. Top the cucumber with a layer of the basil leaves.

✳ Continue the layering, first with the turkey and then with the spinach leaves.

4 roll the wrap

✳ Starting from the edge closest to you, roll up the lavash into a tube.

✳ Using the sharp knife, cut the roll in half on the diagonal.

✳ Serve right away.

the ultimate ham & cheese

makes 2 sandwiches

ingredients

butter 2 tablespoons
all-purpose flour 1 tablespoon
whole milk 1/2 cup
Gruyère cheese 1/4 cup shredded
ground nutmeg 1 pinch
salt
pepper
sandwich bread 4 slices
thinly sliced ham 1/4 pound
thinly sliced Gruyère cheese 1/4 pound

tools

measuring cups & spoons
box grater-shredder
small saucepan
small whisk
wooden spoon
table knife
large frying pan
metal spatula
sharp knife

1 cook butter & flour

* Before you start, be sure an adult is nearby to help. Put the saucepan over medium heat, add 1 tablespoon of the butter, and let it melt. Add the flour and cook, whisking constantly, until the mixture has thickened a little and smells nutty, about 1 minute. Don't let it brown.

2 make the sauce

* Add the milk to the saucepan and whisk very quickly. Reduce the heat to low and cook, stirring constantly with the wooden spoon, until the mixture gets very thick, about 2 minutes. Add the shredded cheese, nutmeg, and a sprinkle each of salt and pepper. Cook, stirring, for 1 minute. Remove the saucepan from the heat.

3 build the sandwiches

* Lay the bread slices in front of you on a work surface. Using the table knife, divide the cheese sauce between 2 of the slices, spreading it evenly. Layer a slice of cheese, 1 or 2 slices of ham, and another slice of cheese on top of the sauce. Top with the remaining bread slices.

4 cook the sandwiches

* Put the frying pan over medium heat and add the remaining 1 tablespoon butter. Let it melt, then tilt the frying pan to coat it evenly. Add the sandwiches. Fry until golden brown on one side. Use the spatula to turn each sandwich to fry the other side. Plan on about 2 minutes per side. Cut in half and serve right away.

more ideas!

ham, cheese & tomato sandwich

Follow the recipe for The Ultimate Ham & Cheese but add ½ teaspoon dried basil to the sauce in step 2. Thinly slice 1 ripe tomato, push out the seeds, and pat the slices dry. Coarsely chop 6–8 fresh basil leaves and sprinkle them over the tomato slices. In step 3, place the tomato slices between the ham and cheese slices. Follow the directions to cook and serve the sandwiches

the ultimate turkey & cheese

Follow the recipe for The Ultimate Ham & Cheese but replace the Gruyère cheese and ham with Cheddar cheese and thinly sliced turkey. In step 2, add ½ teaspoon dry mustard to the sauce instead of the nutmeg. Follow the directions to build, cook, and serve the sandwiches.

ham, cheese & egg sandwiches

Follow the recipe for The Ultimate Ham & Cheese. In step 4, after you melt the butter, crack 2 eggs into the pan and fry until the whites are opaque and the yolks are firm, about 2 minutes. Using the spatula, place 1 egg on each sandwich on top of the ham. Top with the second slice of cheese and bread. Melt another tablespoon butter in the pan and cook and serve the sandwiches as directed.

a layer of cheese sauce makes these sandwiches extra-good!

pb & apple sandwich

ingredients

whipped cream cheese
2 tablespoons

vanilla extract ¼ teaspoon

honey 1 teaspoon

Granny Smith apple 1

**peanut butter, preferably
all-natural** 2 tablespoons

sandwich bread 2 slices

tools

measuring spoons

small bowl

fork

cutting board

sharp knife

table knife

1 mash it together

✳ Before you start, be sure an adult is nearby to help. Put the cream cheese, vanilla extract, and honey in the bowl. Using the fork, mash together until smooth. This could take a minute or two.

2 slice the apple

✳ Ask an adult to help you now. Put the apple on its side on the cutting board. Using the sharp knife, cut the apple in half lengthwise. Then cut each half in half again to make quarters.

✳ Lay each quarter on its side and cut away the tough, papery core and seeds.

✳ Cut each apple quarter lengthwise into thin slices.

3 spread the bread

✳ Using the table knife, spread the peanut butter on one slice of bread.

✳ Spread the cream cheese mixture over the second slice of bread.

4 build the sandwich

✳ Cover the peanut butter with a layer of apple slices, and top with the second bread slice, cream cheese side down. (If you have extra apple slices, serve them alongside the sandwich.)

✳ Press down lightly. Cut the sandwich in half or into quarters with the sharp knife and serve right away.

cheese quesadilla

ingredients

8-inch flour tortillas 2

olive oil or vegetable oil
1 teaspoon

Monterey jack cheese ½ cup
shredded

prepared salsa 2 tablespoons

fresh parsley or cilantro
1–2 tablespoons leaves

Guacamole page 37 (optional)

tools

measuring cups & spoons

box grater-shredder

pastry brush

cookie sheet

oven mitts

cooling rack

cutting board

pizza cutter or sharp knife

1 before you start

✱ Be sure an adult is nearby to help.
Preheat the oven to 450°F. Position the
oven rack in the middle of the oven.

2 build the quesadilla

✱ Using the pastry brush, lightly brush
one side of each tortilla with the olive oil.
Place 1 tortilla, oiled side down, on the
cookie sheet.

✱ Evenly sprinkle the jack cheese over
the tortilla. Dollop small amounts of salsa
over the cheese. Top with the herb leaves.

✱ Place the second tortilla, oiled side up,
on top of the filling.

3 cook the quesadilla

✱ Put the cookie sheet in the oven and
bake until the top tortilla is lightly browned
and crisp looking, 8–10 minutes.

4 cut the quesadilla

✱ Ask an adult to help you remove the
cookie sheet from the oven and place it
on the cooling rack. Allow the quesadilla
to cool for a couple of minutes.

✱ Next, carefully slide the quesadilla
onto the cutting board. Using the pizza
cutter or sharp knife, cut the quesadilla
into 6 or 8 wedges.

✱ Serve right away, with a small bowl
of guacamole for dipping, if you like.

more ideas!

ham & pickle quesadilla

Brush the tortillas with oil as directed for the Cheese Quesadilla. Spread the unoiled side of the first tortilla with 2 teaspoons mustard and sprinkle with ½ cup shredded Cheddar cheese, ½ cup thinly sliced ham strips or diced ham, and thinly sliced sweet or dill pickles. Top with the second tortilla and bake and serve as directed.

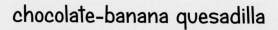

chocolate-banana quesadilla

Brush the tortillas with oil as directed for the Cheese Quesadilla. Spread the unoiled side of each tortilla with 1 tablespoon whipped cream cheese. Top 1 tortilla with 1 small banana, peeled and sliced, and 2–3 tablespoons chopped chocolate-and-almond candy bar. Top with the second tortilla, cream cheese side down, and bake as directed. Sprinkle the top with a little more chopped candy and 1 teaspoon cinnamon sugar before serving.

salami & pesto quesadilla

Brush the tortillas with oil as directed for the Cheese Quesadilla. Spread the unoiled side of the first tortilla with 1 tablespoon prepared pesto and sprinkle with ½ cup shredded Fontina cheese and 4 thin slices salami, cut into ½-inch pieces. Top with the second tortilla and bake and serve as directed.

red, white & green, this version has the colors of an Italian flag

glossary

This alphabetical list explains many of the words, tools, and ingredients you'll find in this cookbook.

a

angel hair pasta

Extra-thin spaghetti. Also called "capellini."

avocado

A buttery, rich fruit that is the primary ingredient in guacamole. Look for Hass avocados that feel slightly soft when gently pressed.

b

bake

To cook with hot, dry air in an oven.

baking potato

A potato with starchy flesh. Russet or Idaho potatoes are the most common.

baking dish

A deep glass or ceramic dish used for baking or roasting.

baking sheet

A rimmed rectangular metal pan used for baking.

balsamic vinegar

Aged Italian vinegar made from wine grapes.

basil

An herb tasting faintly of licorice, commonly used in Italian cooking.

bean sprouts

The sprouts of mung beans. They add a fresh flavor and crisp texture to Asian dishes.

beat

To mix ingredients vigorously, stirring with a spoon, fork, or beaters in a circular motion.

blend

To combine two or more ingredients thoroughly. Also, to mix ingredients in an electric blender.

blender

Small appliance used for blending different types of foods, including dips and smoothies.

boil

To heat a liquid until bubbles constantly rise to its surface and break. A gentle boil is when small bubbles rise and break slowly. A rolling boil is when large bubbles rise and break quickly.

box grater-shredder

A tall, 4-sided metal tool covered with different-sized holes and used for grating citrus zest and for shredding cheese.

broth, chicken

A liquid rich with the flavor of chicken and vegetables.

c

cayenne pepper

Very hot ground red pepper.

chickpeas

Large, beige beans with a firm texture, these are the primary ingredients for hummus. Also called garbanzo beans, chickpeas are easy to find in cans.

chop

To cut food into pieces using a sharp knife. Finely chopped pieces are small; coarsely chopped pieces are large.

cilantro

A distinctly flavored herb used in Mexican and Asian cooking.

cinnamon

The bark of a tropical evergreen tree, cinnamon has a mildly sweet flavor. To make cinnamon sugar, combine 1 part ground cinnamon with 3 parts granulated sugar.

citrus juicer

A shallow bowl with a deeply fluted, inverted cone that fits into a citrus half to easily extract the juice.

colander

A metal or plastic bowl with two handles and many perforated holes, a colander is used to rinse raw foods and to drain cooked foods such as pasta and vegetables.

cooling rack

Made of heavy-duty wire, these square, rectangular, or round racks have small feet that raise them above the countertop. Hot items are placed on top, so that the air circulates on all sides to help the items cool quickly.

coriander seed

A dried spice that adds an exotic flavor to foods, including sauces.

cornmeal

Ground dried corn used to make dough and other bread-like dishes.

cream cheese

A soft, spreadable cheese with a mildly tangy flavor; made from cow's milk. It can be found in a block, or whipped and sold in a tub.

crosswise

In the opposite direction, or perpendicular to, the longest side of a piece of food or a pan.

cumin

A dried spice that adds a smoky flavor to foods.

curry powder

A blend of ground exotic spices commonly used in Indian food.

d

dice

To cut food into pieces that are roughly cubes in shape. The uniform shape helps the food cook evenly.

Dijon mustard

A pungent, yellow-brown mustard that originated in Dijon, France. It can be smooth or coarse-grained, depending on whether the mustard seeds are finely ground or left mostly whole.

dill

An herb with a distinct, sharp flavor. It goes well with salmon and other types of seafood.

dot

To top foods with small bits of butter before cooking. The butter should be scattered evenly over the food for best results.

drain

To pour boiled food, such as pasta or vegetables, into a colander to remove the water. Also used to describe blotting the grease from fried foods on paper towels.

drizzle

To pour a liquid, such as oil, back and forth lightly over food in a thin stream.

dust

To cover a food, your hands, or a work surface lightly with flour.

e

egg noodles

Noodles made with a high proportion of eggs to flour. Perfect for using in soups.

elbow macaroni

Small, short pasta shapes with curves that look like elbows.

f

farfalle pasta

Pasta shaped like bite-sized butterflies or bowties.

fillet

A boneless piece of fish, meat, or poultry.

flour, all-purpose

The most common type of flour available, composed of a blend of wheat. It works well for a variety of tasks.

fontina cheese

An Italian cheese that melts well and tastes slightly nutty.

frying pan

A shallow pan with sloping sides that is used for sautéing or frying food on the stove top.

g

ginger

Fresh ginger looks like a brown, gnarly root and has a refreshing, sweet flavor. Ground, dried ginger has a peppery flavor.

grate

To slide an ingredient, such as citrus zest, across a surface of small, sharp-edged holes on a box grater-shredder to create tiny pieces.

grease

To rub a baking pan or dish evenly with butter or oil to prevent sticking.

green onion

Long, thin young onion with a narrow white base and long, flat green leaves. Also known as a scallion, its flavor is milder than a regular onion.

Gruyère cheese

Type of Swiss cheese commonly used to make cheese sauce.

h

heatproof

Dishes, utensils, or surfaces that can come in contact with high heat without damaging them.

heavy cream

Also called heavy whipping cream, heavy cream has a thick, rich consistency because it contains a high percentage of milk fat.

herbs

Available fresh or dried, herbs are the fragrant leaves and tender stems of green plants.

hull

The tough, white center of a strawberry. Also refers to the process of removing the hull by pulling or cutting it out.

i

instant-read thermometer

A probe-like tool that instantly reads the temperature of a liquid or solid.

k

knead

To work dough with your hands, using pressing, folding, and turning motions. When dough is fully kneaded, it is smooth and no longer sticky.

knife, paring

A small sharp knife for a variety of different uses, including peeling and coring.

knife, serrated

Also called a bread knife, this has a serrated edge that works like a saw to easily cut through the tough crusts of bread or the delicate skins of tomatoes.

knife, sharp

Tool used for slicing, dicing, and chopping all sorts of ingredients. Handle with care!

l

ladle

A small bowl attached to a handle, this tool is useful for serving liquid items like soup or sauce.

lasagna noodles

Large, flat ribbons of dried pasta for layering, sometimes with a ruffled edge.

lavash

Flat, Middle-Eastern bread used to make wrap-style sandwiches.

lengthwise

In the same direction as, or parallel to, the longest side of a piece of food or a pan.

line

To cover the bottom of a pan or dish with parchment paper or aluminum foil to prevent sticking.

m

marinade

Highly flavored, acidic mixture used to flavor and tenderize foods.

marinate

To soak a food in a marinade to add flavor and help tenderize.

meat fork

A large, 2-pronged fork used to steady meat while carving.

mint

A refreshing herb, commonly used in Asian cooking.

n

nutmeg

A fragrant spice ground from the seed of a tropical tree.

o

oil, olive

Flavorful cooking oil pressed from green olives.

oil, vegetable

Bland-tasting cooking oil made by blending vegetable-based oils.

oregano

A pungent herb commonly used in Mexican and Italian cooking.

oven mitts

Thick, heavy-duty cotton gloves that protect hands when handling hot pots or pans.

p

paprika

Spice made from ground dried red pepper, used as a flavoring and for decorating.

parchment paper

A nonstick, burn-resistant paper used for baking.

parsley

A refreshing, faintly peppery herb that is used in a wide variety of different dishes.

parsnip

Similar in size and shape to a carrot, this off-white vegetable has a slightly sweet flavor.

pastry brush

Small brush used for brushing oil on different types of food.

peel

To strip or cut away the skin or rind from fruits and vegetables.

pesto

Italian paste or sauce made from fresh basil, cheese, nuts, and garlic.

pie dish

Shallow round glass or ceramic baking dish.

pinch

The amount of a dry ingredient that you can pick up, or "pinch," between your thumb and forefinger; less than $1/8$ teaspoon.

pita bread

Flat, round bread with a large pocket in the center.

pith

The bitter white part of citrus peel.

pizza cutter

A tool consisting of a rotating wheel attached to a handle that easily and safely cuts pizza and other flat foods into serving pieces.

potato masher

Specialized tool that makes it easy to smash boiled potatoes and other soft fruits or vegetables.

preheat

To heat an oven to a specific temperature before use.

r

red pepper flakes

Also called crushed red pepper, this spice adds hotness to dishes.

rice noodles

Noodles made from rice flour and water, popular in Asian cooking. They can be found in a variety of different widths.

ricotta cheese

A loose, mild, cow's milk cheese commonly used to make lasagna. It is sold in plastic tubs.

rise

What happens to a dough or batter when it becomes bigger as a result of the gas released by the yeast the dough contains.

roast

To cook with hot, dry air in an oven.

roasting pan

A large rectangular metal pan with handles for cooking in a hot oven.

rolling pin

A long wooden tool used for rolling out dough.

roll out

To flatten dough with a rolling pin until smooth, even, and usually thin.

room temperature

The temperature of a comfortable room. Recipe ingredients are often brought to room temperature so they will soften and blend easily.

rosemary

An herb with a strong, fragrant, slightly woodsy flavor, commonly used in poultry and meat dishes.

s

saucepan

A pan with tall sides used for cooking on the stove top, such as simmering soups and boiling pasta.

sauté
To cook food over high heat in a small amount of oil or butter using a shallow pan.

sauté pan
A shallow pan with straight sides used for cooking food on the stove.

season
To add salt, pepper, or other seasonings to food little by little, stopping and tasting until it is to your liking.

sesame seeds
Pale tan, small, flat seeds used as a topping or coating.

set aside
To put ingredients to one side while you do something else.

shallot
A small, mild, onion-like vegetable with bronze or reddish skin.

shred
To cut an ingredient, such as cheese, on the medium or large sharp shredding holes on a box grater-shredder.

simmer
To heat a liquid to just below boiling. The surface of the liquid should be steaming and a few tiny bubbles may form.

sizzle
A vigorous bubbling of oil accompanied by a hissing sound, which signals that the heat in a pan is sufficient for cooking.

slice
To cut food lengthwise or crosswise with a knife, forming thick or thin pieces.

soy sauce
A popular Asian sauce that adds deep, salty flavor to food.

spatula, metal
A thin metal tool attached to a long handle used for turning food as it cooks.

spatula, rubber
A flexible rubber tool attached to a wooden handle for scraping the sides of mixing bowls. Also available are heatproof spatulas made from silicone for scraping hot foods.

spread
To apply a soft item, such as mayonnaise or butter, over another food in an even layer.

stir
To move a spoon, fork, whisk, or other utensil continuously through dry or wet ingredients, usually in a circular pattern.

sugar, brown
A moist blend of granulated sugar and molasses. Brown sugar is sold in two basic types: light (also known as golden) and dark.

sugar, granulated
Small, white granules that pour easily. When a recipe calls for just "sugar," always use granulated sugar.

sweet potato
Sometimes called a yam, this sugary vegetable has either yellow-brown skin and yellow flesh or dark reddish or purplish skin and dark orange flesh.

t

tahini
A paste made from sesame seeds often used in Middle Eastern cooking.

tartar sauce
A sauce used to accompany fish and shellfish made from mayonnaise, pickles, and other flavorful ingredients.

Thai fish sauce
An extremely pungent, highly flavorful condiment used in Southeast Asian cooking.

tender
Describes food that is cooked until it is soft enough to cut and chew easily, but is not mushy.

thicken
When a food changes from a loose, liquid consistency to a thick, firmer one.

tongs
Scissor-like tools with blunt ends for grasping food.

trim
To cut food so that it is uniform in size and shape. Also, to cut away any unneeded or inedible part.

V

vegetable peeler
A small tool used for stripping peels off vegetables and fruits.

W

whisk
A whisk is made of loops of sturdy wire that are attached to a handle. To whisk something means to stir a liquid vigorously with a whisk, adding air and thereby increasing its volume.

Worcestershire sauce
A dark, thin, pungent sauce used to flavor sauces and meats.

work surface
A flat space, such as a kitchen counter or a kitchen work table, used for cutting, mixing, or preparing foods.

y

yeast, dry
Microscopic plants that, when activated, make pizza and bread dough rise.

z

zest
The thin, brightly colored outer layer or peel of a citrus fruit.

index

*f*P

FREE PRESS

A Division of Simon & Schuster, Inc.
1230 Avenue of the Americas
New York, NY 10020

WILLIAMS-SONOMA

Founder & Vice-Chairman Chuck Williams

WELDON OWEN INC.

Chief Executive Officer John Owen
President and Chief Operating Officer Terry Newell
Chief Financial Officer Christine E. Munson
Vice President International Sales Stuart Laurence
Vice President and Creative Director Gaye Allen
Vice President and Publisher Hannah Rahill
Associate Publisher Sarah Putman Clegg
Senior Editor Jennifer Newens
Art Director and Designer Marisa Kwek
Production Director Chris Hemesath
Color Manager Teri Bell
Production and Reprint Coordinator Todd Rechner

WILLIAMS-SONOMA KIDS IN THE KITCHEN SERIES

Conceived and produced by Weldon Owen Inc.
814 Montgomery Street, San Francisco, CA 94133
Telephone: 415 291 0100   Fax: 415 291 8841

In collaboration with Williams-Sonoma, Inc.
3250 Van Ness Avenue, San Francisco, CA 94109

A WELDON OWEN PRODUCTION

For information regarding special discounts for bulk purchases,
please contact Simon & Schuster Special Sales at 1-800-456-6798 or
business@simonandschuster.com

Set in AG Schoolbook, Arial, Candy Square, Gill Sans and Joppa

Color separations by Bright Arts Hong Kong.
Printed and bound in China by Toppan Leefung Printing Limited.

First printed in 2006.

10 9

Library of Congress Cataloging-in-Publication data is available.

ISBN-13: 978-0-7432-7856-0
ISBN-10: 0-7432-7856-9

Author

STEPHANIE ROSENBAUM has been a food writer and cookbook
author 15 years. She has contributed to *French* and *Soup & Stew* in
the Williams-Sonoma Collection series and *Baking* in the upcoming
Food Made Fast series, also from Williams-Sonoma. She is also
the author of *Honey from Flower to Table*. Her articles have appeared
in numerous publications including *San Francisco* magazine and
Vegetarian Times. Ms. Rosenbaum lives in Brooklyn, New York, where
she cooks, writes, teaches, and publishes an online cooking
column, *Adventures of the Pie Queen*.

General Editor

CHUCK WILLIAMS, general editor, has helped to revolutionize
cooking in America. He opened his first Williams-Sonoma store in
the California wine country town of Sonoma in 1956, later moving
it to San Francisco. More than 235 stores are now open in the
United States, and the company's catalog boasts an annual
circulation of more than 40 million.

Photographer

JASON LOWE is an award-winning food and travel photographer.
His work has appeared in numerous magazines and cookbooks,
including *Savoring Tuscany; Savoring Provence; Essentials of Grilling;
Kids Baking;* and Foods of the World *Barcelona* and *Florence;* all are
volumes in Williams-Sonoma cookbook series.

ACKNOWLEDGMENTS

Weldon Owen wishes to thank the following people for their generous
support in producing this book: Heather Belt; Geoff, Tara, and Ella Brogan;
Cate Conniff; Ken DellaPenta; Leslie Evans; Sharon Silva; Bob and Coleen
Simmons; and Sharron Wood. We would also like to thank our wonderful kid
models: Eliza and Guy Beca; Thomas Bedford; Holly and Maddison Brogan;
Jammel Liuaga; Sasha McEwen; Freddy Riddiford; and Zildjian Talaepa.

recipe list